The Bindery Tea

Journal

of

haiku and senryu

Autumn 2020

Submissions

Please go to poetrypea.com to check the deadlines and topics for submission to future journals.

Copyrights, Views

All prior copyrights are retained by contributors. Full rights revert to contributors upon publication in T*he Poetry Pea Journal of haiku and senryu*. Poetry Pea retains the right to publish the work on social media, and the poetrypea website www.poetrypea.com, with proper citation. Poetry Pea editors assume no responsibility for the views of any contributors whose work appears in the journal, nor for research errors, infringement of copyright, nor failure to make proper acknowledgment of previously published material.

Contents

Introduction 1

Voyages 2

Winter bites- a renku 24

Joy 28

The Secret Valley of the Elves 56

Loss 68

Contributors 95

Introduction

Welcome to the *Poetry Pea Journal of haiku and senryu, Autumn edition*. Thanks for all your wonderful contributions and your support for this project.

Poetry Pea aims to build a community of haiku poets of different levels from the beginner to the highly accomplished, to learn from one another in a supportive and positive way and to spread the joy of haiku.

In this journal you'll read haiku and senryu on the topics of *Voyages, Joy* and *Loss* as well as the renku *Winter Bites*. There is also a chapter dedicated to submissions received following my presentation at the Haiku Society of America's Zoom conference *The Haiku Pea Podcast Live: Inspiration - Walk with me in the Secret Valley of the Elves*. You too can experience the virtual walk via YouTube at the Haiku Society of America's YouTube channel.

Some of the poetry included here has been read on the *Haiku Pea Podcast*, but others are written only for this journal. I hope you'll be inspired to write and submit to the next one. To find out more, please go to poetrypea.com.

Patricia McGuire, editor

Voyages

The Judge's Choice

rainy morn'
my never-ending trip
on the wrong bus

Nisha Raviprasad

This haiku appeals to me because of what isn't said. The image of a rainy morning and trying to catch a bus and you get on the wrong one. There you sit while the bus winds slowly, in and out of suburbs, stopping and starting while your stomach is churning because you are getting ever further from your destination. You check your watch, and a feeling of dread overcomes you as the image of the confrontation with the boss and your possible explanations enters your mind. The rain and a dismal overall feeling of gloom expressed in 'rainy morn' completes the picture.

This haiku has an effective simplicity about it as well, which attracted me for its dedication to the haiku genre.

Community Judge: Giddy Nielsen Sweep

travel in Covid
atlas pages in colour
imagine me there

mermaid beneath the sea
what brings merman so deep?
sailor's net cast far

Laura Lynn Driscoll

strolling footpaths
discovering treasures,
such splendour

Serlina Rose

storm-split trees
a meandering river
finds the estuary

Alison Lock

strands of curly hair
follow different paths
of a broken compass

summer sun,
I pass by my old self
on the gravel road

Kelli Lage

where oceans collide
poverty and wealth entwine
redolent of home

Shaun Temple Brown

summer snow-storm
dandelion seeds in flight
seek a place to rest

Sarah Connor

through my window
toward sunshine dreaming
childhood long ago

Melody O'Neil

one more candle blown
marking my voyage
around the sun

hungry seeds
inside ripened fruits
awaiting voyage

S Narayanan

travel ban -
my mind wanders
in our past

crossing the border
I change a word
in my haiku

    Andrea Cecon

                      soft pink petals float
                      whisked by spring winds to water
                      covering for streams

                            Matthew Weigelt

where we are going
none of us know, yet onward
we trek together

journey to a land
far and deep and high
my home above

    Linda L Kruschke

                      beautiful day
                      walking from the house
                      to the car

                            Michael Baribeau

a kaleidoscope
of fractured dreams
coming back together

Sarah Calvello

farmlands, failing towns
quivering in miles of haze -
no where to go

Elder Gideon

sudden rain -
a baby spider climbs
my neck

Rachel Magaji

behind their time zone
I think of the ones I love
asleep tomorrow

fewer and fewer
of us fly south for summer
migratory birds

Jane Berg

winding dad's clock
i travel back
to childhood

ancient temples and
satellite dishes
along the Nile

Jenni Wyn Hyatt

morning mist
eyes on the summit
onward we march

summer scorch
watching the alpine peaks
daydreams melt

Zahra Mughis

on a pirate ship
whichever way the wind
you are a pirate

daring to set out
makes a big difference
home sweet home

Lana M'Rochel

a scent of lemon -
twilight gilds
the Fontana di Trevi

road to the beach -
on the boat in gold,
Bottoms Up!

Elaine Wilburt

tears and swash
first voyage into my soul
that was always veiled

Moumita Ghosh

night camp
a mosquito flying
into the fire

Rahma Jimoh

solo cloud said Italy;
heart envisions Eire -
   azure dream sky

starboard east wind roars chill fear

Wayne Kingston

car park -
in every windscreen
the sun

Máire Morrissey-Cummins

building an ark
the countless voyages
of carpenter pencils

wendy c bialek

first view of the sea boketto

vacationing
in my spring hat
the spider

Roberta Beach Jacobson

night train -
wide awake in a cradle
a smiling child

early flight
at the boarding gate
the sun arrives

Srinivas S

power line
my bus and a dense fog
travel together

pre-vacation rites -
he calls my handy
in search of his keys

    D V Rozic

                  portage
                  from lake to lake
                  loons

                  escape from the world
                  on the Galveston ferry
                  terns in flight

                          Deborah P Kolodji

loading the car
full moon breaks through
my busyness

colonial square
sunset gives way to light
bathed facades

    Craig Kittner

across the paving
ants dance a winding pattern
to birdsong

arriving by air
the silver birch
I didn't order

Elaine Patricia Morris

driving
through freezing fog
a story unfolds

Roger Watson

morning departure
warning whistle blows
through the daisies

Kate Alsbury

mediterranean
coral craft bargains
sign language

Christina Chin

silent today
hay rattle seeds
by the roadside

    Dr Tim Gardiner

raining in Paris
the tower stands above me
what an eyeful

city by the lake
cuckoo clocks and chocolate
fondues and farewells

    Sarah Bint Yusuf

eastern bazaar
in the voice of the saleswoman
spicy notes

with open mouth
dreaming of travel abroad
a suitcase at the door

    Bakhtiyar Amini

a journey
to the moon and back
late-night jazz

    Tiffany Shaw Diaz

promenade deck…
three walking sticks
pass me by

sé de Lisboa -
the beggar taps his phone
on the steps

Marilyn Ward

changing wind…
a suitcase ready
in the hallway

at dawn
greeting my parents…
chirp of swallows

Daniela Misso

ashes on the water
bon voyage flowers
— her final trip

Linda L Ludwig

hometown streets
smaller than I remember
my childhood

m shane pruett

tucked in
i sail away to the stars
hot water bottle

sailing away
the leaf boat dad made for me
water under the bridge

James Young

                                        I find myself
                                        strolling through the grass
                                        open spaces

                                                    Katherine E Winnick

lake mist dawn
the slow pull of oars
through my thoughts

shorts and shades
stepping off the plane into
the thermal scan

John Hawkhead

matriarch
train leaving the station
left with thoughts of yore

Richard Bailly

winter's gone
the migratory flamingos
flying back home

the willow tree
waiting for a flock of herons
returning home

Bhawana Upadhyay

woodbines - choking up on Ellis Island

Pacific Blue
on the flip side
a forever stamp

Lovette Carter

rosebay willow-herb
and dandelion clocks -
abandoned railway platform

Peter Draper

heading out to sea
moon and stars' reflections
bioluminescence

    Richard Hargreaves

        Insomnia…
        the plane's wing lights
        blinking blinking

            Isabel Caves

train to Agra
my friend points out
my unpolished nails

    Neelam Dadhwal

        cold night
        the voyages
        of stars

        halfway
        up the hill -
        lady beetle

            Pearl

sunday night train
stowing the weekend
in the overhead

Bill O'Sullivan

abroad
how we search the city
for our selves

Jonathan Roman

city exodus
a moving van
covered in graffitti

absinthe bar
the Arles light posts glow
in Van Gogh green

Jay Friedenberg

honey bees
collect shadow pollen
dark side of the moon

neck pillow
walks the airport
end to end

Erin Castaldi

divorce papers
the winding road
to loneliness

Willie R Bongcaron

singing 'Let's Fly Away'
while packing
the zip's tight groove

Mark Gilbert

Cliff Richard
ringing in our ears
summer holiday

Bisshie

contrails
the undulation of dunes
becoming water

Debbie Strange

after migration
a shady resting station
busy bird feeder

Barbara Carlson

arches of sunlight
   slipping below the waves
. . . dolphins

cold sips of coffee
rain on the gangplank
and a woman's song

eddy lee

we begin and end
in unknown outstretched hands
life's journey

Robert Quezada

summer stream
an ant sails past
on a leaf

photo
a castle in France
and my thumb

David Oates

rough sea
every minute a new wave
of nausea

Vandana Parashar

a voyage of
a thousand words
— sorry

        Jason Furtak

bright lightning flash
then rumbling through the valley
loud thunderous boom

        Rob McKinnon

dead fly
the steady train
of ants

        Nisha Raviprasad

simply walking
through the cold mist
no end in sight

his groundless fear of flying

        Robert Horrobin

happiness and rainbow
floating flower
somewhere above me

        Eva Drobná

unfolded map
all the places beyond
my wallet

Rashmi VeSa

                          fresh breeze
                          on the ferry rail
                          my school satchel

                          wild waves -
                          making sense of the ship's
                          safety instructions

                                        Dorothy Burrows

combat adventures
with chosen comrades in arms
voyages of youth

        Andrew Syor

                          souvenir
                          of a sea voyage
                          salty lips

                                        Kim Russell

white feather
carried from river to river…
so far that ocean

Lavana Kray

butterfly
from flower to flower
to my suitcase

Mariela Coromoto

maiden voyage
she tries not to collide
with the other kid's boat

grand voyage
a pod of playful dolphins
on the starboard bow

Tracy Davidson

urging me
to move on
cathedral bells

end of the diary
waiting for dawn
three empty boats

Richa Sharma

voyage of discovery
she reads his
personal diary

Anjali Warhadpande

                                              on the windswept moor
                                              a mare flies after fancies -
                                              untameable mind

                                                              Mark Morris

long drive home -
the prairie disappears
behind us

hot-air balloon
floating still higher
the day moon

        s zeilenga

Winter bites- a renku

The poets who joined me in writing this renku: James Young (JY), Giddy Nielsen-Sweep (GNS), Ian Speed (IS), Michael Baribeau (MB), Bisshie (B)

    winter bites -
    in my rice bowl
    only tears

JY

        scratching the snow
        a squirrel's hoard

B

    found food functions
    better than exotic recipes
    and fancy dining

IS

        no feet of clay for this
        plodding house wife

GNS

    flower moon
    a coolness creeps
    into the harrowed soil

B

        slaked limestone
        life's bitter sweetness

JY

    my kiln belly
    anticipating the crop
    i plough on

JY

        hunger for bitterness leaves
        upturned earth unsweetened

IS

    kissed by summer
    asleep in the bee meadows
    a trout stream

JY

        in the frying pan
        hibiscus flowers float

GNS

    color tour
    a thermos for tea
    to warm our hands

MB

        plucking clover
        for its nectar

B

pollinated
infusing
the red petals

        IS

    a moth circles
    around the moon's reflection

        B

starlight
caterpillars feasting
on nasturtiums

        JY

    the rabbits left me
    one garden tomato

        MB

in the spotlight
table roses and stew
run bunny run

        GNS

    dew drops
    on the leftovers

        B

sunrise
sipping coffee
together

B

    plates wiped clean
    mug empty sunset alone

IS

kintsugi
the porcelain dish beneath
the last few candies

MB

    donburi friends
    breaking bread in golden times

JY

Joy

The Judge's Choice

shaking
the raindrops out of the tree...
childhood

Diana Salusia

This verse grabbed my attention from the start.

The first line is a surprise. No traditional seasonal references or scene setting here; the poet takes the reader straight to the heart of the action, with the verb 'shaking'. For me, this word effectively captures the physical sensation of being so deliriously happy or so profoundly scared that your body just can't be still. In two syllables the poet has hooked my interest. I want to know who is shaking and why.

Then the second line tells me more. It is not particularly dramatic; raindrops are being made to fall from a tree, an occurrence that perhaps most people will have seen and can relate to. Put the first and second lines together and I think an intriguing scene begins to form. I imagine leaves shivering; sense water dripping. I picture a long tree branch because the second line is long, containing seven of the eleven syllables. The short beats of these words increase that sense of motion. I can see and feel this moment, but I still don't know who is making that tree tremble.

And then, in the final line, all is revealed: a child or a group of unknown children are shaking a branch and, in doing so, having fun. It is an everyday incident with a universal resonance. But the poet's choice of the word 'childhood 'presents an unexpected metaphor. It makes me pause and think. Is there a connection between shaking raindrops from a tree and childhood?

On reflection, I think there is. For me, this image beautifully captures the energy, curiosity and playfulness of being young and alive. Again, the second line is pivotal to this. The succession of short syllables mirrors how children relentlessly look, experiment, are adventurous and curious; ask question after question until they find the answers. These tree-shaking children are living in the moment, learning how to fathom the world and to make things happen through play: what greater joy could there possibly be?

Community Judge: Dorothy Burrows

I measure distance
in smiles per nautical miles -
this kiss is beaming

so sweet
that joy that is almost
pain

    Karla Linn Merrifield

        raindrops
        seeping into me
        a love ballad

        in this lifetime
        a new sound -
        baby's coo

        Richa Sharma

record scratch
I chortle at
his dance moves

the tapping of paws
draws nearer
I am home

    Kelli Lage

grandpa's shadow
sitting from across him...
moonlight tales

rose red...
the deep colour
of afterglow

   Taofeek Ayeyemi

      crying tears
      of joy
      the new mother

        Laura Lynn Driscoll

a love letter
signed in italics
"Your Fool"

   Bakhtiyar Amini

      sunny drizzle -
      your zest
      my lemon cake

      her gift
      tied with care and ribbon -
      dandelion

        Dorothy Burrows

olives
scattered over the path…
sharing sun

smiling…
in his eyes
a rainbow

    Daniela Misso

                          geishas silk
                          painted red lips - sigh
                          artificial joy

                          warm summer sun
                          shines on her face
                          her smile

                                  Linda L Ludwig

shy grasshoppers
hiding in the tall grass
while mating

a cowgirl tossing
her smile, as if I might
get away

    Rp Verlaine

tears turning to rain
footprints become memories
puddles of joy

    Michael Feil

        double rainbow
        how long before we find
        it within ourselves

        palpitations
        ...the dull ache
        of first love

            Vandana Parashar

priory ruins glow
vibrations kiss air hugged skin
emerald body floats

    Katy Simpson

        picked together
        they taste even better -
        blackberry hunt

            Diana Salusia

soap bubbles
a boy chases
his laughter

4 a.m.
my mother and I share
a cup of tea

Veronika Zora Novak

fistful of sweets
today I am
a kid at heart

Tiffany Shaw Diaz

first rain…
children jump and dance
naked

August rain…
farmers in the market
offloading yams

Owolabi Awwal Olanrewaju

the sweetest of spots
sound of willlow
on leather

Jeff Brake

first day of school
the excited chatter
of starlings

afternoon birdsong -
the air full
of blossoms

Marilyn Ward

                                      downpour
                                      a little girl's laughter
                                      runs in circles

                                      first love
                                      dancing to the music
                                      of her smile

                                                    m shane pruett

evening breeze…
my niece lets me
pinch her cheeks

temple ghat
floating diyas lighten up
the dusk

Neelam Dadhwal

Sunday in Paris -
children's boats float
in the pond

best friends -
at recess collecting
four-leaf clovers

      Elaine Wilburt

                pediatric ward
                becoming a father
                for the nth time

                at long last
                no more sleepless nights…
                school project

                        Willie R Bongcaron

touching grass
for the first time -
toddler toes

finally old enough
to eat wherever I want -
crackers in bed

      Julie Bloss Kelsey

crossing the line
plumes of coloured smoke rise
with the cheers

    Michael Kitchen

'yesterday'
impromptu karaoke
after dinner

    Dr Tim Gardiner

unknown melody
unheard lyrics
yet the heart soars

    Anjali Warhadpande

Beethoven's ninth
the children try to stop
giggling

breaking waves
the rise and fall
of cheetah skin bikini boobs

    Jay Friedenberg

festival tulips
frolicking and tossing
jealous honeybees

August night
crickets pleasing symphony
a woman discos

    Bhawana Upadhyay

        shostakovitch two
        movement one climactic phrase
        chills up and down spine

            Richard Bailly

ah, the smell
of fresh ground coffee
...this morning's enema

    wendy c bialek

        out of the darkness
        something special is brewing
        first tea of the day

            Sarah Bint Yusef

one-by-one blueberries

part of
my morning landscape
cows

    Roberta Beach Jacobson

        sweetness of wild fruit
        summer on wetted lips
        juices of sipped sin

            Richard Hargreaves

red-stained fingers
and painted lips
cherry tree bounty

two worlds blend
spicy and hot
kismet

    Barbara Carlson

        boiling honey
        a scent of warm orange blossoms
        permeates the house

            Kevin Flanagan

unstoppable
the mint wafer
urge

confetti
on her wedding day
a rain of cherry blossoms

Christina Chin

wind chimes -
the joy of
reading haiku

cloudburst shocks -
burnt peach tree shoots
pale pink blossoms

Neera Kashyap

a whiff of wind -
the cucumber leaf
waves hello

butterfly net -
chasing words
for this haiku

Valentina Ranaldi-Adams

windowless room
a book of haiku
takes him outside

in his wheelchair
leading like a general
before his troops

    David Oates

                      concert
                      in all our chests
                      the same song

                      fireflies
                      the words on the page
                      begin to shine

                                  Jonathan Roman

monsoon morning
inhaling the aromas
of wind blown dreams

within pages the secret life of a bookworm

    Rashmi VeSa

evening breeze
in the backyard
a ball chase

midnight latte
some roasted peanuts
and a sonnet

    Zahra Mughis

    british racing green
    polished paintwork shiny chrome
    1964 MGB

    Rob McKinnon

my white knuckle ride
he drives over Jackson Heights
joy in his eyes

    Elaine Patricia Morris

    banners and kleenex
    in every hand -
    troops returning home

    joyfully piling up
    the bones
    Sunday fried chicken

    Lorraine A Padden

golden afternoon
I kiss your little
buddah belly

she hums happily
as I blow dry her hair
Autumn morning

    Melissa Patterson

        happier than the bride
        her great-grandmother
        catches the bouquet

            Tracy Davidson

my joy
disappearing with
the rainbow

twilight years…
the joy of turning in
early

    Jason Furtak

        sun beams behind leaves
        sparkling on my teeth

            Riham El-Ashry

closed lids fluttering sun and shadow leaves

a day somewhat cooler
the cat returns to his spot
on my chest

Craig Kittner

                                                spring
                                                old walk
                                                brand new leaves

                                                stumbling from
                                                window to roof
                                                wild moon chase

                                                            Jane Berg

fully naked
in Lake Ontario -
mesmerized by fish

trees with
love carvings
heal themselves

       Garret Schuelke

the milker cows
in a slow plodding line
my four year old eyes

halfway up the tree
I consider
my next move

    Giddy Nielsen Sweep

        peonies in bloom
        the ants
        get carried away

        heavenly sky
        I climb the ladder
        of an old pine

        Kristen Lindquist

the sun shines
the flower captures
smiles everywhere

    Lekha Desai Morrison

        picnic basket
        picking some wild flowers
        to see her smile

        Cyrille Soliman

a voice so clear calls
to my peace at the moment
nirvana comes near

flowers for August
in the full sun that makes sure
they become pure bliss

Veronica Eisert

                                            meditation time
                                            and i am writing
                                            poems instead

                                            catching
                                            a dandelion seed
                                            the thrill of possibilities

                                                              Mike Rehling

in the fields
buttercups brush my legs
with stardust

gladdening
murky waters -
kingcups

Jenni Wyn Hyatt

poppy field red alert
stretching beyond seeing
lost in its oneness

Ian Speed

                              a child's smile
                              tugged by the wind
                              sky full of kites

                              pink peony
                              opens to the sun
                              a geisha's lips

                                          Kim Russell

dragonfly lifts me
its wings in sunlight reveal
a web of bright truth

        Beth Cusack

                              sun erupts into day
                              dragonfly wings
                              ignite the air

                                        Robert Quezada

windowpane
I touch my fingers
to a butterfly

flower child
the bee becomes a part
of her skirt

    an'ya

the way the breeze
catches the lilacs…
a breath of morning light

morning shadows
and then suddenly
a butterfly

    Angela Terry

no butterfly
but a spent yellow leaf
just as beautiful

    Mike Gallagher

gravity has
no hold on the sky-lark's
spiraling song

    Hannah Hulbert

tail wags
he picks up
the leash again

I didn't notice
the butterfly that
landed on me

    S Narayanan

        seven days
        from chrysalis to yellow wings
        seven days

        bumblebee napping
        — simple happiness
        in an open bloom

        B A France

a lady bug
on the boc choi -
dancing wind chimes

noon day sun
cupped in the center
of a daisy

    Carrie Ann Thunell

home at last
a baby turtle
dives into the ocean

Rajeshwari Srinivasan

                        still pond
                        the coot chicks
                        near grown

                        between
                        sleep cycles
                        full moon

                                  Pearl

dog tongue hanging
wind-blown ears flapping
out a car window

little wren hops
with giant voice sings
cheerup chip chip chip

Linda L Kruschke

                        unlocking sound
                        behind the door
                        a wagging tail

                                  Tomislav Sjekloća

wild angelica
the candied scent
of your name

sun trap
the cat's tail tickles
my toes

Debbie Strange

                              on this full moon night
                              a scattering of stars
                              brings the shadows to light

                                          Fiona H

seeing the comet
i throw my hat in the air
it lands first

i read a poem
and the words start laughing
at my smile

        James Young

                              shadows from the clouds
                              provide relief from the sun;
                              breathe in the beauty

                                            RJ Tungsten

corn tide winds
spiralling out of indigo
her love whispers

midnight bay
beyond the shingle
our stepping-stone stars

John Hawkhead

power cut -
the joy of shadow birds
in the candle light

the earth
speaks its ecstasy -
petrichor

Srinivas S

sliver of blue sky
after yesterday's grey day
a magic carpet

colorful toys
abandoned in sunshine
for ice cream

Trey Treeful

plump cloud vapor
            drifts
bright cerulean
            canvas
summer quilting

Wayne Kingston

           perfume of wine -
           remembering the bouquet
           she gave me once

           filling emptiness
           waves dance over each other -
           the sky meets the sea

Professor R K Singh

tiny spring
flows freely along the trails
calm trickle

Serlina Rose

           liberated
           by summer heat
           a rivulet's joy

Paul Callus

at one with nature
seasonal observations
from my balcony

Andrew Syor

                our quiet paddles
                spawning lines of small eddies
                into dusky lake

                wild barley -
                blonde hair blowing
                in a prairie wind

                          Art Fredeen

backyard
filled with visitors
butterflies

vista point
those few moments alone
with the horizon

Deborah P Kolodji

                joyous moment
                the scent of summer
                on the sea breeze

                          Katherine E Winnick

flowering apple tree
the joy of pollination
honey bees

Eva Drobná

tilt left
careen to the right
first two wheeler

Maggie Roycraft

The Secret Valley of the Elves

In July 2020 I was honoured to be invited to present a talk at the Haiku Society of America's Zoom conference. I presented a walk through the Lauterbrunnen valley in my home country of Switzerland. This valley was visited by JRR Tolkien before he wrote his books *The Hobbit* and the *Lord of the Rings Trilogy*. He based the Elven home of Rivendell on his wanderings in this area.

I invited those who had been at the conference and those who had viewed the video by the end of July 2020, to submit haiku inspired by our walk. As you are reading this, it's too late for you to submit, but if you would like to take a walk with me in the valley you can still see the presentation on YouTube on the Haiku Society of America's channel. In the meantime, I hope you enjoy the haiku inspired by the walk. My thanks to all the poets who wrote some terrific work after our trip. I think we are all honorary Elves, don't you?

remembering
the rucksack
on the decline

Bruce J Pfeffer

far corner of the school library
discovering Tolkien

the quiet in the pines
across the field
away from the house

Matt Snyder

trillium glade
I decide
to follow
the deer trail

Dianne Garcia

crooked shed
leaning deep
with the mountain

Lori Becherer

the math teacher
loses count . . . 72
waterfalls

 Mimi Ahern

 narrow view
 the waterfall separating
 as it falls

 the spread of moss
 on boulders
 our slow ascent

  Deborah P Kolodji

river ford
carefully placing
one boot after another

where the trail
escapes the trees
the shape of the sky

 Angela Terry

 waterfall thread
 moss pads
 the sheer walls

  Anne Elise Burgevin

wild water spilling down alpine flowers

on the mountain path
between rock walls
losing my shadow

  Adelaide B Shaw

      iPad turned off
      I talk to the lily pads
      better reception

      late spring snow melt
      the waterfall
      already rushing

        Sari Grandstaff

mountain river
the flow of our
small talk

wading through the stream
where your ripples
reach mine

  Edward Cody Huddleston

first light
cowbells echo
in the mist

mountain pass
hiking side by side
with an endless sky

    Bona M Santos

              cleft in the valley
              draws me
              into the mist

              village steeple
              dwarfs
              distant mountain peaks

                      Janice Doppler

taking a break
then another break
summit brook

whitewater rapids
no birds only the thunder
of tumbling water

    Christina Chin

my rucksack heavier
on the downhill
the path's little treasures

below the peaks
green velvet meadows
hide elfin homes

Linda L Ludwig

whispers
behind the rocks
mountain brook

crystal clear
a tarn gathers
clouds

Paul Callus

high summer
the icy river
we don't swim in

spiderwebs
a maze of branches
off the trail

Agnes Eva Savich

willow tree
the river flows past
rustling its leaves

lazy day
i decide
to name the breeze

   Mike Rehling

        waterfall
        the clouds arrive
        at my feet

        rainbow mist
        hanging on the waterfall
        morning sunshine

           James Young

frozen river
the cracking
of smiles

dawnbreak -
falling rain
with birdsong

   Nicky Gutierrez

sandals in one hand,
crossing the shallow river;
feeling eternal

Ian Richardson

       early spring walk
       i stop and look again
       jack-in-the-pulpit

       stories about elves
       after the campfire's loud snap
       silence

       Michael Baribeau

echoes of wind
a familiar voice
speaks to me

walking alone -
the shadow sketches
the edge of light

Pravat Kumar Padhy

       alpine lake voice
       haunting echoes popping groan
       stretching water

       Wayne Kingston

bells ring
out of the mist
the face of a cow

on a pine log
we share lunch
& a fly's insistence

      Doris Lynch

          mountain climb
          boots fill with snow
          the child cries

          walking holiday
          each step takes you a little
          further away

                Jane Berg

spring thaw
trickle trickle
fall

      Brenda Lempp

          bridge crossing
          branches veil the path ahead
          beyond knowing

                Trey Treeful

silent mountains
the packed cable car ride -
ten languages

alpine trail
the steep path ends…
wildflower meadow

    Christine Wenk-Harrison

        Waterfall -
        hiking down into
        the valley's story

        as a waterfall
        loses itself in a pool -
        the sound

            Richard Tice

thick moss
on a blackrock wall
    crow bones

cool evening…
the faint scent of rain
    and woodsmoke

    Brett Brady

silence…
filtered through spruce
the gold of sunset

mountain stream
cracks through the glen -
edelweiss

      Kathleen Tice

      no room for the virus
      Alpine mountains
      giving breath

            Maureen L Haggerty

mist
the top of the mountain
missed

      Dana Grover

      between birch branches
      we play hide and seek
      the moon and I

            Maggie Roycraft

crystal waterfall
mountain's braid
blows in the wind

grass on the roof
the snowfinch sees
an empty valley

    Amanda N Butler

chaotic beauty
uncontrolled cohesion
white on green

    Mark Farrar

Loss

The Judge's Choice

reading her journal
a day too late
all the signs

Tracy Davidson

Loss is a topic that covers a wide range of emotions deepened by what has been lost. There are losses that are minor, like losing our car keys, or where we may have lost our eye glasses. Some losses are merely perceived, like feeling emotionally lost due to circumstances. Life circumstances change and we feel a loss, but continue on our journey. The worst loss is the death of someone we love, and our grief is deep and very real!

I chose this haiku, by Tracy Davidson, as it speaks to not only the loss of someone special from our life but of their death by their own hand. We see that what seemed to be such an unexpected event was, in fact, planned. The levels of feeling are so far reaching: and if I'd known maybe I could have stopped it; why didn't I see their sadness or pain; how could they not have shared those feelings with me, and so on...

I think this hits home with most people as many of us seem to know of a person who has taken their own life, only to find out their lives weren't as happy and successful as they seemed.

This haiku, in a minimal number of words, shows loss, grief and revelation. This poem moved me in its simply stated grief.

Community Judge: linda l ludwig

between funerals
I pause
to repair my lipstick

grey pigtail
beneath his coat
a rented coffin

    Joan Barrett

                  wind
                  in the wildlife park
                  ashes

                  a ruin crumbles
                  into its footprints
                  development

                        Christina Chin

pallbearing
the weight
of what's already gone

kintsugi bowl
her new family heirloom

    Lorraine A Padden

grave site -
we help each other
cross the ice

    Janice Doppler

        daybreak -
        at the graveside
        quarrelling with his wife

            Samo Kreutz

breaking waves
I keep writing the name
they erase

    Vandana Parashar

        prolonged ringing
        I brace to hear
        your voicemail

            Kelli Lage

elements
devour the names
set in stone

    Hannah Hulbert

broken lotus root
these threads of longing
for my former self

haiku habit
counting syllables
in his goodbye note

Jackie Chou

memorial service
a bird soars high
in the gathering dusk

Bona M Santos

the blue jay and sparrow
share a tiny tombstone
storm damage

Barbara Carlson

do not ask why
just say goodbye
release with love

technology whiz
going to memory care
ram malfunction

Richard Bailly

numb
she washes the sheets
shattered motherhood

Tracy Davidson

                      plum
                      falls on ground
                      miscarriage.

Rose (s bharti)

obituaries
she learns the adult bio
of her high-school sweet heart

miscarriage
still searching for her child
inside herself

Maya Daneva

                      onion peeled
                      endless illumination
                            haiku weeps

Wayne Kingston

empty nest -
something of me
in the waning moon

arvinder kaur

lone sheep
finding a place
outside the flock

battered nest
all my siblings
in the wind

Jonathan Roman

Alzheimer's
unexpectedly she plays
childhood piano tune

her wrinkled face
inside a gilded frame
my nightly tears

Giddy Nielsen Sweep

will we remember
jumping to the endless sounds
of youth going wild?

Bryan Myers

it's Christmas
no lights... no tree
widow's weeds

hot steamy night
she lies cold -
in his absence

      Linda L Ludwig

              seven years on
              the echoes of my screams
              die too

                    Richard Hargreaves

homesick
scent of sunlight
in mother's hair

      Veronika Zora Novak

              on the terrace
              facing the sun
              an empty chair

                    Professor R K Singh

her red bra
long after she left it

thunderstorm
feeling more alone
even the cat disappears

Rp Verlaine

strings of beads
in the pawn shop window…
endless rain

piano practice -
what my fingers
no longer remember

Angela Terry

slanted sunlight -
swing shadows sway
on the fence

waning moon -
first a cane,
then a walker

Elaine Wilburt

summer rain
trying to remember
grandma's voice

    Tomislav Sjekloća

evening surf -
footprints trace
new waterlines

sandy shoreline -
forgotten buckets
bring back memories

    Bill Fay

all the verbs
in what no one knew
was his death poem

childhood home
putting my memories
on the market

    Jennifer Hambrick

summer rain
no voice remains
but a face

    Bisshie

patchy mist
on the mountain
cataracts

estate sale
closing down
a life

      Valentina Ranaldi-Adams

                              thinning salmon run
                              the fishing trip
                              that never was

                              even as we talk
                              of childhood friends
                              winter rain

                                          Richard Tice

man's best friend
the water dish -
still full

      Laura Lynn Driscoll

                              instead of
                              a headstone
                              your dog bowl

                                          Jane Berg

fireflies
one by one
go dark

    Bob Carlton

        late summer
        the evening shortens
        to a blackbird's call

        in a cardboard box
        the little wax doll
        sleeps

            Marilyn Ward

lying by the path
a bird's dry dusty body
the silent dawn

    Patrick Stephens

        the cry of the gull
        high above empty sand dunes
        low autumnal tides

            Sarah Bint Yusef

ibis circling
in thick morning fog
white on white

    Dawn Toomey

        silent spring
        i can still see
        the birds

            Robert Horrobin

i admire
the lovely fish tank
eating sushi

    S Narayanan

        by the road
        armadillo's shell
        all his plans

            David Oates

incomplete smile
the tooth fairy
drops her shiny coin

    Cyrille Soliman

empty nest -
embroidering doves into
my days

pillow talk -
my son asks for a pound
from the tooth fairy

Dorothy Burrows

                family album
                closing my eyes
                your smile

                old age home
                the leaves fall
                with no noise

                              Neena Singh

ah, this complex life
inevitable losses
necessary gains

    Andrew Syor

                sometimes
                her voice on a breeze
                a feather

                                Kim Russell

a sand Buddha
only the head is left
by the waves

a sex-shop
an old man
deplores his life

Bakhtiyar Amini

bomb blasts
doll survives
lifeless hands

Anjali Warhadpande

a bruise upon a bruise - sayonara

summers pastimes

James Young

raindrops cling
to the autumn haws -
drip-feed

he dumps his hiking boots -
summits
he'll never climb

Peter Adair

nowhere town
a refugee looks for himself
in the temple pond

broken nib
the i's and the j's
lose their heads

Srinivas S

night train
the window reflects
the rain inside

Zahra Mughis

crescent moon
my empty arms
a broken plate

Eve Castle

dressed in rags
deft little fingers
stitch garments

Lekha Desai Morrison

camouflaged -
nestling in shingle
my missing keys

    Jenni Wyn Hyatt

        picking up a stone…
        the red rock country
        only a memory

        revised resume
        letting go
        of old dreams

            Kathleen Tice

becoming
another adult
another adult

staring at soap suds finding no pattern

    Alex Fyffe

        lost keys
        i retrace
        my steps

            Pearl

unplugging from the
world is not the world's loss -
it is yours

    Ian Speed

              prisoner's night
              the low walls
              of remorse

              child bride
              the crushed petals
              of a plucked flower

                    Rashmi VeSa

when
the postman retires
who will speak to me

porch light
on for you until
the bulb burns out

    Roberta Beach Jacobson

              isolation
              the rainy day
              is silent

                    Rajeshwari Srinivasan

unpacked groceries
the missing loaf
of bread

a week after
the mastectomy
bra commercials

    Deborah P Kolodji

        couch on the curb
        someone takes
        the "FREE" sign

        granny's rocker
        in front of the TV
        still

            Dan Burt

no funeral urn
a cheerios box
for my ashes

fog
and the sound of
lost birds

    Mike Rehling

gamble for a rush
poker, baccarat, craps, slots
time to get more cash!

human touch
a hug or a handshake
please

    RJ Tungsten

        daybreak -
        the world wallows
        in disaster

            Willie R Bongcaron

from her car
a masked friend waves
falling cherry blossoms

last erratic breaths the wind chimes fill in

    Doris Lynch

        the magpie surveys
        empty city sidewalks
        faces behind glass

            Trey Treeful

solitaire with sushi
lingering over
the pickled ginger

reaching for a face mask
the feel of summer
alters

Craig Kittner

front line casualties
nurses
replace soldiers

my throat
closing
the family photo album

Ronald K Craig

missing
the friendly obscenities
of the workplace

remembering
only the footfall
our last date

Mike Gallagher

at night we lie there
staring at the ceiling fan
regrets float on air

    Bruce Lomas

        much to confess pale dawn

        diagnosis
        a pigeon pecks
        at a dry leaf

            Richa Sharma

dead wind -
she opposes
reconciliation

    Paul Callus

        open door
        the streetlight casts a glow
        on an ending

        the road is bent
        freedom waits
        out of sight

            Sarah Mahina Calvello

this morning
I choose solitude
Amaryllis

    Dr Tim Gardiner

    cloud shadow
    passes over the sundial
    in real time

        Maggie Roycraft

a green leaf
cast in the shade
no voice

    Riham El-Ashry

    poppy seeds burn
    summer dreams in
    the smokey kitchen

    granny knits
    missed a drop stitch
    his faded scarf

    long dry summer
    the willow branch doesn't
    reach the river

        Robin Rich

leaf buds
the beech finally lets go
of last year's leaves

fresh snow
only the top
of Buddha's head

   Kristen Lindquist

      falling leaves -
      the weight of each
        life

      death valley
      the vibrance of flowers
      in low places

         m shane pruett

banks deposit dirt
into the swollen river
withdrawing ground

   Beth Cusack

      one colour
      covering the garden
      winter

         Damir Damir

dry lake bed
the rainy season's
unresisted path

 Erin Castaldi

    in my hair
    the wind of waves…
    summer dream

     Daniela Misso

a swing
the old branch creaks
back and forth

 Anna Maria Domburg-Sancristoforo

    moonflowers
    cool wind of twilight
    …dawn approaches

     B A France

dutiful routine
new flowers
for old

 Rob McKinnon

a tree's
last breath…
paper stars

river dusk
the lightness
of your ashes

Isabel Caves

        the sun surrenders
        to an awaiting sea
        night and you are gone

        Robert Quezada

deadheading roses
accidental bee run-in
one less bee

Linda L Kruschke

        heavy rain
        weeping willow
        weeping

        JP Meredith

orchid
how calmly you leave
this earth

        Tiffany Shaw Diaz

                winter jasmine
                we inhale the scent
                of dying stars

                        Debbie Strange

soaking up
the now...nothing goes
down the drain

        wendy c. bialek

Contributors

My thanks to the following poets who wrote wonderful haiku, monoku and senryu for this journal.

Peter Adair	Anne Elise Burgevin
Mimi Ahern	Dorothy Burrows
Kate Alsbury	Dan Burt
Bakhtiyar Amini	Amanda N Butler
an'ya	Paul Callus
Owolabi Awwal Olanrewaju	Sarah Calvello
Taofeek Ayeyemi	Barbara Carlson
Richard Bailly	Bob Carlton
Michael Baribeau	Lovette Carter
Joan Barrett	Erin Castaldi
Roberta Beach Jacobson	Eve Castle
Lori Becherer	Isabel Caves
Jane Berg	Andrea Cecon
wendy c bialek	Christina Chin
Sarah Bint Yusuf	Jackie Chou
Bisshie	Edward Cody Huddleston
Julie Bloss Kelsey	Sarah Connor
Willie R Bongcaron	Mariela Coromoto
Brett Brady	Ronald K Craig
Jeff Brake	Beth Cusack

Neelam Dadhwal
Damir Damir
Maya Daneva
Tracy Davidson
Lekha Desai Morrison
Anna Maria Domburg-Sancristoforo
Janice Doppler
Peter Draper
Laura Lynn Driscoll
Eva Drobná
Veronica Eisert
Riham El-Ashry
Mark Farrar
Bill Fay
Michael Feil
Kevin Flanagan
B A France
Art Fredeen
Jay Friedenberg
Jason Furtak
Alex Fyffe
Mike Gallagher
Dianne Garcia
Dr Tim Gardiner
Moumita Ghosh
Elder Gideon

Mark Gilbert
Sari Grandstaff
Dana Grover
Nicky Gutierrez
Fiona H
Maureen L Haggerty
Jennifer Hambrick
Richard Hargreaves
John Hawkhead
Robert Horrobin
Hannah Hulbert
Rahma Jimoh
Neera Kashyap
arvinder kaur
Wayne Kingston
Michael Kitchen
Craig Kittner
Deborah P Kolodji
Lavana Kray
Samo Kreutz
Linda L Kruschke
Pravat Kumar Padhy
Kelli Lage
eddy lee
Brenda Lempp
Kristin Lindquist

Alison Lock
Bruce Lomas
Linda L Ludwig
Doris Lynch
Lana M'Rochel
Rachel Magaji
Sarah Mahina Calvello
Rob McKinnon
JP Meredith
Karla Linn Merrifield
Daniela Misso
Elaine Patricia Morris
Mark Morris
Máire Morrissey-Cummins
Zahra Mughis
Bryan Myers
S Narayanan
Giddy Nielsen-Sweep
Veronika Zora Novak
Melody O'Neil
Bill O'Sullivan
David Oates
Lorraine A Padden
Vandana Parashar
Melissa Patterson
Pearl

Bruce J Pfeffer
m shane pruett
Robert Quezada
Valentina Ranaldi-Adams
Nisha Raviprasad
Mike Rehling
Robin Rich
Ian Richardson
Jonathan Roman
Serlina Rose
Rose (s bharti)
Maggie Roycraft
D V Rozic
Kim Russell
Srinivas S
Diana Salusia
Bona M Santos
Agnes Eva Savich
Garret Schuelke
Richa Sharma
Adelaide B Shaw
Tiffany Shaw Diaz
Katy Simpson
Neena Singh
Professor R K Singh
Tomislav Sjekloća

Matt Snyder
Cyrille Soliman
Ian Speed
Rajeshwari Srinivasan
Patrick Stephens
Debbie Strange
Andrew Syor
Shaun Temple Brown
Angela Terry
Carrie Ann Thunell
Kathleen Tice
Richard Tice
Dawn Toomey
Trey Treeful

RJ Tungsten
Bhawana Upadhyay
Rp Verlaine
Rashmi VeSa
Marilyn Ward
Anjali Warhadpande
Roger Watson
Matthew Weigelt
Christina Wenk-Harrison
Elaine Wilburt
Katherine E Winnick
Jenni Wyn Hyatt
James Young
s zeilenga

Thank You

Thank you to everyone who submitted to the haiku pea podcast and to the *Poetry Pea Journal of haiku and senryu*. There wouldn't be one without you.

My thanks to Giddy Nielsen Sweep, Dorothy Burrows and Linda L Ludwig, who gave up their time to be community judges and write such interesting and enlightening commentaries.

James Young and Robert Horrobin were wonderful guest editors for the podcast and the journal, thank you both.

Maggie Roycraft, thank you so much for your editing and design advice. I think it's made a difference to the quality of the Journal. I've certainly learnt a great deal by working with you.

Last but definitely not least; thanks to Jonathan Roman, Harry, Imogen, Leo and to Maggie Roycraft. Where would I be without my extra eyes? Thanks so much for checking through the proof copy.

Until the next journal… keep writing!

Patricia

Made in the USA
Coppell, TX
09 December 2020